MW00769470

I Love You,
Mom

We gratefully acknowledge the permission granted by the following authors to reprint their poems or excerpts that appear in this publication: Susan Polis Schutz for "Having You in My Life Made Growing Up a Little Easier." Copyright © 1983 by Stephen Schutz and Susan Polis Schutz. All rights reserved. And Paula Finn for "Where Would I Be Without You?" Copyright © 2016 by Paula Finn. All rights reserved. And Jason Blume for "Life goes by...." Copyright © 2004 by Jason Blume. All rights reserved.

ISBN: 978-1-59842-979-4

⋔ and Blue Mountain Press are registered in U.S. Patent and Trademark Office. Certain trademarks are used under license.

Printed in China.
First Printing: 2016

♻ This book is printed on recycled paper.

This book is printed on paper that has been specially produced to be acid free (neutral pH) and contains no groundwood or unbleached pulp. It conforms with the requirements of the American National Standards Institute, Inc., so as to ensure that this book will last and be enjoyed by future generations.

Blue Mountain Arts, Inc.
P.O. Box 4549, Boulder, Colorado 80306

I Love You, Mom

A Blue Mountain Arts® Collection

Edited by Becky McKay

Blue Mountain Press™

Boulder, Colorado

Thank You for Being My Mom

Mom, every time you read this, I hope you'll remember... that I can't even imagine a more wonderful mother than you.

I want these words to help me give you the most heartfelt thanks I have ever said to anyone. Thank you for all the sweet, abundant things you do and the generous ways you contribute to my life.

The light that shines in you has always been there to illuminate the path in front of me, and there isn't a day that goes by without my life being warmed by yours. Thank you for your wisdom, encouragement, steady support, and constant love.

With all my heart, thank you for being a more priceless gift than words can express. Thank you for being my mom.

— Douglas Pagels

Where Would I Be Without You?

You gave me such a healthy, happy start in life, and you have encouraged me steadily ever since. You're the one person I've always trusted completely to respond with a helping hand and an open heart to my smallest and greatest needs.

You raised me to think independently, create passionately, and dream boldly. I never felt pressure to be exactly like you or model my life after yours. You gave me the freedom to form my own style, build my own skills… and discover what makes me happiest.

You never expected me to be perfect. You understood that a little rebellion is part of growing up and mistakes are part of learning.

You showed me how to make the most of the good times and to face the difficult times with courage. I've watched you build strength from weakness and transform setbacks into chances to succeed. You've gained something positive from every experience — good or bad — and inspired me to do the same.

Your influence is the root of all my strengths and the reason I've grown up to be confident, capable, and happy with my life.

— Paula Finn

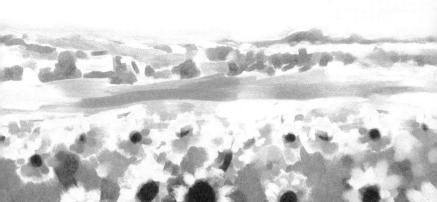

When I was a child, I didn't
understand how hard you worked
to provide everything
you wanted me to have.
Some might say that's a parent's job.
But looking back,
I know you did so much more
and gave so much more
than you needed to.
And you did it with so much love.

You put your own needs aside
to care for me.
Now that I'm an adult,
I understand how you sacrificed,
and I know how lucky I am
to have been blessed
with such a wonderful mother.

— Jason Blume

It's an Honor
to Call You My Mom

I have shared a relationship with you
since the moment I was born. The bond
between us is enormous, and though
sometimes it's not perfect, it's something
I can always count on when it feels as if
everything else is falling apart.

I'm so glad that God in His infinite
wisdom allowed me to belong to you —
to be your child and your friend. More
than anything, I'm so thankful to have
been given the honor to love you and
call you my mother.

— Pamela Malone-Melton

You Are So Many Wonderful Things to Me

You are my role model extraordinaire.
You are my source of sage advice.
You are my wise counsel for all
the best things I've learned about life.
You are my traveling companion,
lovingly beside me on the way
to all my tomorrows.
You are a guardian angel
with hidden wings.

You are the best support system imaginable.
You are wide-open arms, enfolding hugs,
and the loveliest smiles I'll ever know.
You are everything I admire in a person,
and you are what unconditional love
is to me.

— Chris Gallatin

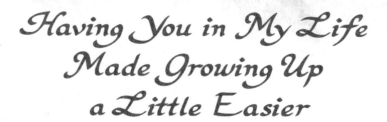

Having You in My Life Made Growing Up a Little Easier

When you have a mother
who cares so much for you
that anything you want
comes before her desires
When you have a mother
who is so understanding that
no matter what is bothering you
she can make you smile

When you have a mother
who is so strong that
no matter what obstacles she faces
she is always confident in front of you
When you have a mother
who actively pursues her goals in life
but includes you in all her goals
you are very lucky indeed
Having a mother like this
makes it easy to grow up
into a loving, strong adult

— Susan Polis Schutz

I Will Always Need You

No matter how old I get,
I'll still need to hear you say
you're proud of me.
I'll need your advice,
even though I may not take it.
I'll need to know how you are —
even when you don't feel well
or would rather not "burden" me
with your problems.
No matter how busy I get,
I'll always need to hear you say
you thought of me today.
I'll need to hear your voice,
even if I may not have
enough time to talk.
I still need to know you love me.

No matter how upset I am,
I'll always need to hear you say
that you know I can handle it.
I'll still need to hear
your honest opinion,
even though it might annoy me.
I'll want to know about
your experiences,
even if it takes me years
to learn from them
or to apply that knowledge
to my own situations.
No matter what's going on in my life...
I will always need you.

— Gail Dickert

Ten Great Things About You, Mom

- You know just what to say to cheer me up.

- You inspire me to be a better person.

- You give great hugs.

- You tell me you love me and are proud of me.

- You taught me about life, love, and pursuing my passions.

- You gave me the gift of life.

- You are a great example of what it is to be a parent.

- You comfort me when I'm sad and share in my joy when I'm happy.

- You believe in me with all your heart.

- You are always there for me, no matter what.

Everyone Should Have a Mom like You

Everybody needs someone
to love them in a special way —
to hold them through life's storms,
share all that's in a day,
offer a shoulder to lean on,
and be there to care.

Everybody needs someone
who shares their heart's concerns,
who'll listen as no one else can or will,
who'll consider their concerns seriously
and offer the most thought-out advice,
who will think of only the very best.

Everybody needs someone to love them
    in a special way.
I only wish everyone had someone
as special as you.

— Barbara J. Hall

I've Looked Up to You All My Life

Time after time, you are the one
who proclaims your pride in me,
but now it's my turn to talk of pride
and place the spotlight on you —
for the life you've lived
and the example you've been to me.
No matter the situations life has dealt,
you've handled them with honor and grace.
You are a woman of countless abilities.

I've looked up to you all my life;
growing up, I assumed you could
    do most anything.
The pride I have in you goes beyond
all the things you have done.
I'm proud of the person
    you've always been —
kind, caring, dependable, and wise.
So now I am the one who is bragging…
because, Mom, you just make me so proud!

                 — Cheryl Barker

You've Always Been by My Side

In my growing-up years,
   we went through so much together as
      a team.
You made my life your own,
   sacrificing your happiness for mine.
You never gave up on me.
You simply stood by me,
   reassuring me that I would make it
   through any obstacle that came my way.

There were times when tears filled my eyes
    and I was filled with doubt,
but during those times when I was
    most fragile,
you were the steady rock that kept me
from falling apart.
You were so strong and loving,
so sweet and kind.
You've given me far more
than I ever deserved,
and I truly don't know
what I would do without you.
My heart is full of happiness
all because of you —
because of your joy,
because of your love.

— Shannon M. Dickinson

The Best Parts of Me Are from You

If I'm strong, it's because you've shown
me how to handle problems without
being overwhelmed by them.
If I'm gentle, it's because you held
me close when I was sad and quietly
waited with me while life leveled out.
If I use my sense of humor, it's because
you've taught me to laugh and keep
life's challenges in perspective.

If I'm independent and confident, it's because
you let me know it was all right to have
my own thoughts and make my
own choices.
If I'm compassionate, it's because you have
shown me the importance of caring about
people rather than possessions.
If I'm loving and passionate, it's because you
have shown me your love through all the
ups and downs of growing up and
growing away.

I'll try never to forget that the best parts of
me are from you.

— Judith Hintz Tanaka

When I Look at You, I See Life, Love, and So Much More

When I look at you, Mom, I see my life through your eyes. I see the strength you always offer me, the comfort you continuously show me, the support you provide me, and the magnitude of the love that you unselfishly share.

I see the tears you shed when I cry, the laughter you share when I laugh, the hope you have for me when I feel disillusioned, and the faith you have in me when I face life's challenges.

I see the many sacrifices you have made and continue to make for me, the inspiration you are to me when I need direction, the devotion you show me as a parent, and the encouragement you give me when I need a friend.

When I look at you and see my life through your eyes, I feel loved.

— Susan Hickman Sater

I Am Forever Grateful for You

You held my hand through all my life,
found patience and understanding
when I made the wrong choices,
praised me in all my moments of success,
and taught me how to give
to others from the heart.

You protected me when I was afraid,
sheltered me from danger,
allowed me to grow and create dreams,
and encouraged me
to bring those dreams to life.
You never gave up on me,
never walked away from me,
and never let me live one day of my life
without feeling special.
Thank you for loving me so much
and for giving me the best of you.
I will never live a day of my life
without being grateful.

— Debra Heintz Cavataio

Thoughts of You Never Fail to Brighten My Day

You are a person who
    believes in life's bright side.
I know, because you've helped me
    to find it many times.

You are someone who considers
    another's feelings first.
I know, because you've always
    cared for mine.

You are a friend who will stop
    everything else to listen,
to be a special source
    of understanding,
and to offer hope and help
    in any way you can.
I know, because you've always
    been a guiding light for me.

Just thinking of you
    has the power to
        brighten up my day.

— Barbara J. Hall

You're an Inspiration to Me... and to Everyone Who Knows You

Everything you do is done in the spirit of sharing and caring and making your corner of the world a better one. When people think of you, they think of a helping hand, a loving heart, and one of the sweetest people on the planet. I am in awe of your strength, your gentleness, and all the blessings you bring to the people who are lucky enough to be in your life.

You sacrifice and support and give so much of yourself. And I have to imagine that if you're sometimes a little tired at the end of the day, it's only because you have gone so far out of your way to make life nicer for everyone else! You are good and kind and generous and wise and wonderful. You are amazing.

— Ann Turrell

You Are a True Blessing

When I count my blessings, I think of you, Mom. You give me encouragement and hope. When I don't know which way to turn, many times you know the right thing to say to keep me going.

I am glad that I have your wisdom to guide me. It is very easy to talk with you, and you are a dear friend as well as a wonderful mom. You will never know how much our conversations mean to me.

It is comforting to know you are there. I don't tell you often enough how much I depend on you and how much I appreciate your love and support. You have taken care of me, and you continue to strengthen me so that my life is richer and fuller.

I hope that my life will reflect love, strength, and patience as yours does. I love you more each day, and I am so happy that I have a wonderful mother... one who makes my world a brighter place with her love.

— Shirley Welsh

I Love You, Mom, with All My Heart

*N*o words can describe the depth of my feelings for you.

Just thinking of you can bring a tear to my eye, a smile to my face, and the most thankful feeling I'll ever have… to my heart.

Your love is what sees me through more things than you'll ever realize. I cherish our closeness, just like I've treasured every generous, giving, understanding, and supportive thing you've ever done for me. The list goes on and on, and I'm not sure I could ever count all the things you've done that have made a difference to my heart and to my happiness.

There have been so many times when you have felt just like a gentle sunrise shining for me, sending wonderful wishes my way, warming my soul, inspiring my days, and lifting up my spirit.

Mom, you are just too wonderful
        for words.

But I want to say this anyway,
        because you deserve to hear it:

        I love you
                and I always will
                        with all my heart...

                forever.

                        — Ceal Carson